Daycare and Diplomas

Daycare and Diplomas

Teen Mothers Who Stayed in School

by the students at South Vista Education Center

Fairview Press • Minneapolis

Published by Fairview Press, 2450 Riverside Avenue, Minneapolis, Minnesota 55454.

Library of Congress Cataloging-in-Publication Data
Daycare and Diplomas: teen mothers who stayed in school / by the students at South Vista Education Center.
    p. cm.
    ISBN 1-57749-098-3 (pbk.: alk. paper)
      1. South Vista Education Center (Richfield, Minn.) 2. Pregnant schoolgirls—Education—Minnesota—Case studies. 3. Teenage mothers—Education—Minnesota—Case studies. 4. Teenage parents—Education—Minnesota—Case studies. I. South Vista Education Center (Richfield, Minn.)

LC4092.M46 S68 2000
306.874'3—dc21   00-037620

First Printing: January 2001

Printed in the United States of America
05 04 03 02 01   7 6 5 4 3 2 1

Cover: *Cover design by Laurie Ingram Duren*™

Photographs for Fairview by Len Larson

Publisher's Note: Fairview Press publications, including *Daycare and Diplomas,* do not necessarily reflect the philosophy of Fairview Health Services.

For a free current catalog of Fairview Press titles, please call toll-free 1-800-544-8207. Or visit our web site at www.fairviewpress.org.

To the students of South Vista Education Center,
who inspire us daily with their strength,
their courage, and their determination.

Acknowledgments

Major funding and support for *Daycare and Diplomas: Teen Mothers Who Stayed in School* comes from the Fairview Foundation, Fairview Health Services, and Midwest Coca-Cola Bottling Company.

Thanks also to the people who made this book possible:

Mary Baich, executive director of Fairview Foundation and former director of Fairview Community Health Outreach

Nancy Bengston, formerly of South Vista Education Center

Ann Bergmann Ewing, program facilitator at South Vista Education Center

Francis N. Crisman, Ph.D., director of Area Learning Center of Intermediate School District 287

Krista Ditscheit, Fairview Community Health Outreach intern

Karen Hoglund, Children and Family Services of Hennepin County

Rose Jost, RN, PHN, MEd, of Bloomington Division of Public Health

Len Larson, photographer

Linda A. Packard, director of Fairview Community Health Outreach

Barbara Jean Pederson, RN, PHN, BSN, of Bloomington Division of Public Health

Barbara Reilly, RN, PHN, BSN, of Bloomington Division of Public Health

Mark Vukelich, former director of Fairview Public Relations

Daniel Weber, vice president of Fairview Southdale Hospital

Contents

The Students

The Partners

A Community Unites

In Minnesota, thirteen babies are born to teenage mothers every day. In Hennepin County alone, one out of thirteen babies is born to a teenage mother. In fact, statistics across the country show a growing concern over teen pregnancy and parenthood, yet society has been slow to address the issue.

Many businesses, for example, avoid hiring teen parents because they are unwilling to face the complexities involved. And according to the National Education Association, educators, too, tend to ignore teenage pregnancy, assuming that pregnant students will simply drop out of school. Some educators even pressure students to leave.

Pregnant students who leave school often intend to return after the baby is born. But the challenges of teen motherhood make this difficult, sometimes impossible. In fact, only 50 percent of mothers under age eighteen graduate from high school. To stay in school and succeed in life, these young people need the support of family, the educational system, and the medical system.

Fortunately, there are organizations dedicated to helping these teens finish school, prepare for a career, and become resourceful parents. For example, in Hennepin County, Minnesota, a partnership has formed between Intermediate School District 287, Bloomington Division of Public Health, Hennepin County, Fairview Southdale Hospital, Fairview Community Health Outreach, the Fairview Foundation, and Fairview Health Services. These partners work to provide a comprehensive educational program in a supportive atmosphere. Together, they are helping teen parents succeed in their education, career goals, and family life.

Even with extensive support, however, pregnant and parenting teens endure stresses well beyond those of their peers. In addition to tests, homework, and term papers, they face issues of nurturing, childcare, medical appointments, and other parenting concerns. Unfortunately, teen mothers often confront these challenges without assistance from the child's father.

Teen parents face serious economic problems. They must provide for themselves as well as their children, but because they are students, they have little time to work. Without a high school diploma, teen parents are unable to find jobs with adequate pay and flexible hours, making it difficult to attend to their children and complete their high school education.

Teen parenthood is not glamorous. It is an exhausting responsibility, and few teenagers have the economic and emotional resources to do the job alone. By encouraging these young people to stay in school, by providing daycare, healthcare, parenting classes, family planning assistance, and other essential services, we give teenage parents a chance to raise healthy, well-adjusted children *and* complete their education.

The stories in this book are success stories. Each of these students describes—in her own words—her fears, her uncertainties, and the obstacles she has overcome as a parent or pregnant teen. Each student is determined to stay in school, to follow her dreams, and to build a successful life—for her child, and for herself.

FRANCIS N. CRISMAN, PH.D.
Director of Area Learning Center of Intermediate School District 287

Ann Bergmann Ewing

Preface

When asked to write an essay for this book, the young women at South Vista Education Center jumped at the chance to be heard. They are eager to tell you what has happened to their lives. After receiving all the best advice about teen parenting, they now have an opportunity to share their experiences and offer their own advice.

Their stories consistently portray the awe with which they have watched their lives take an unexpected turn. Some of these young women took risks; others were victims. All will attest that becoming a teen parent is intensely stressful. And yet, despite their hardship, these young mothers draw a driving inspiration from their children, inspiration that pushes them to find support, continue their education, and build their future.

At South Vista Education Center, we greet these young women daily as they bring themselves and their children into school. We sigh when we note who is absent, because we know that a spirit has been weakened by poor health, family stress, academic frustration, teenage distractions, or sheer exhaustion. We call on the community to help provide support services, and we persist because these young mothers have told us that they want to succeed as parents. What a gift to themselves, their children, and our communities when they do.

ANN BERGMANN EWING
Program Facilitator at South Vista Education Center

The Students

Jessica and her son, Austin

Jessica

~

If a normal teenager lived a week in my shoes, she would think twice before having a child. Becoming a parent means that another human comes before you. You are not number one anymore!

As a teenage mother, you take on more responsibilities than most adults can handle. I am a full-time mother, full-time high school student, and part-time worker. In addition, I completed a certified nursing assistant (CNA)course and will be starting a trained medication aide (TMA) course in a month.

My day usually begins at 5:30 A.M. From then until 7:00 is basically the only ninety minutes I will have for myself all day. Austin, my son, wakes up around 7:00. Twenty minutes later we board our little yellow school bus. School starts at 8:10 A.M. and lasts until 2:25 P.M. Our after-school ritual is to eat a snack and watch *Teletubbies.* I try to focus all of my attention on Austin for this hour and a half before I leave for work. He is in the care of others almost all day and needs some tender loving care from me. My job usually consists of two five-hour shifts during the week and two seven-hour shifts on the weekend. Bedtime for me is usually around 11:00 P.M.

This may sound like a heavy load for one person to handle, but I am not alone. My wonderful mother has always been there for me, offering strength, support, and love. Without her, Austin and I would not be as close and loving toward each other.

Having paid daycare is also a big help, so I can continue my education. They provide Austin with a nurturing environment and encourage his development.

Kehara and her son, Tyrell

Kehara

~

I could feel a change in my body that made me think I was pregnant. So I finally convinced myself to take a pregnancy test. When I found out I really was pregnant, I was in denial. I was thinking, *No, this can't be happening to Kehara, not Kehara.*

When I got up the guts to tell my mom, she was very hurt and disappointed. She had so many hopes for her daughter, a straight-A student with a 4.0 grade-point average. And now my whole life was going to be thrown away. So my mom wanted me to have an abortion. She looked at the situation as though she had to kill her grandchild to save her child's life. Eventually, she realized that it was not right. She could not ask me to kill my child, because she could not kill her own child. So we decided to keep the baby.

Being a parent at age fifteen is something I never thought would happen to me. But it did. I have sacrificed a lot by having my son, but I would not trade him for the world. Tyrell is everything I expected him to be, and much more.

The hardest parts about being a parent are waking up in the middle of the night, going to school after staying up with the baby most of the night, and just not knowing what tomorrow may bring.

My son's father, also named Tyrell, is very much in his life. He is supportive, responsible, unselfish, caring, loving, and everything a father should be.

My son is now two months old, and he is my pride and joy. I love him and his father with all my heart. I really can't figure out how I ever lived without my son. He makes me feel complete. I have to finish school, not only so I can have a future, but so my baby can have one, too.

Alison and her daughter

Alison

~

Being a parent is the best and hardest thing I've ever done. It's challenging; every day I wonder if I'm doing the best or the right thing for my daughter.

Pregnancy was a lot harder than I thought it would be. I felt tired, sick, weak, and miserable the whole time. Labor and delivery weren't as bad as everyone told me they would be. I think being well-informed really helped.

The hardest thing about being a mother is giving up my social life and extracurricular activities. Before I had a baby, competition squad was a big part of my life; now it's out of the question. I hardly ever get to go out anymore. I wouldn't trust just anyone to watch my daughter, and babysitters are expensive. Babies are expensive, too—diapers, formula, bibs, clothes, toys, and other needs—and it's hard not having much money anymore.

I've never been as happy in my life as I am now. Before, I was unhappy and angry and didn't have any goals for my life. My daughter changed all that. I love every day with her, and now I have a lot of goals for the future. I never used to care about school, but now I realize how important education is. I want to provide a good life for myself and my daughter. I never really got along with my family before, because I was too busy getting into trouble and hanging out with my friends. I'm lucky to have such a good family; they are all so supportive. My boyfriend is also very supportive, and he's really good with the baby.

My daughter teaches me to be more patient and tolerant. Babies have their own agenda; it takes a lot of patience to deal with them. Because of her, I've also learned how to communicate better. It's amazing how much I've learned from my four-month-old baby—and to think that I have many more months to go.

It seems like she does something new every day—smiling, cooing, turning over, grabbing things, starting on solid foods—I have so much fun watching her, I just love it. Before I had her, whenever I got sick I would lie in my bed and sleep. Now, I just look at my daughter's smile and I forget that I'm sick, because she makes me so happy.

I've always loved kids, but I never planned on having a baby this early. It's overwhelming and exhausting, but I wouldn't change it for the world.

Casey and her son, Jessie

Casey

~

People should know that being a teen parent is stressful. You have to deal with school issues, family issues, and then the issues with the baby. I love being a mom. Everyday is a new adventure, but an exciting one.

I got pregnant when I was fourteen years old and had Jesse when I was fifteen years old. Taylor, his dad, told me that if I got pregnant he would stay with me. Taylor has not been there for us since he found out that I was pregnant and that I was going to keep Jesse.

While I was pregnant people told me I should do this or I should do that. It was very confusing. I wanted to keep my baby but also my family. I ended up doing what I had wanted to do all along—keep him.

Jesse is very active and on the go constantly. I love him more than anything in this world and I'll do anything to keep him safe, even if it costs me my life and happiness.

Hang and her son, David

Hang

~

For me, being a parent is very hard. I need to make all the decisions about how to raise my child. I have to learn to be patient, loving, and caring. Discipline will be the hardest part, because he is my baby and I love him. I have to learn how to manage money so I have enough for my son's needs. I haven't had time for myself because I spend most of my time with my son. I have noticed that I don't have time with my friends.

Every morning I wake up at 6:00 A.M. and I take a shower. Then I eat breakfast and get all of my stuff ready to go. At 6:45 I have to wake my son, David, who doesn't like to wake up. He usually cries and screams, and I don't like that. At 7:25 I have to go to the front door and wait for the bus. Some days it is so hard to get ready, and I'm always rushing to get things done.

When I get to school, I have to get my son into his daycare, which is at my school. Then I have seven classes to go to. At lunch break I usually go see my son, who loves to see me. I feel great when I see him, when he gets excited. When it is time to go home, I have to get my son and get on the bus. This is what I do every day, and it is very hard to do every day.

When I get home from school, I get my son ready to eat a snack. Then I read him a book for fifteen minutes. Then I pop in a movie for him to watch while I'm getting dinner ready. This takes me at least one hour and thirty minutes. We have dinner when my mom comes home from work, usually around 6:30 P.M. From 7:15 to 7:30 I give my son a bath. Then at 8:00 I get him ready to go to sleep, and I usually read to him. After he goes to sleep, I have one hour to myself. I usually watch a movie or just sit down and relax. Every day I feel very stressed out. Having a child when you are young is very hard. It is even harder when you have an aggressive child, like mine.

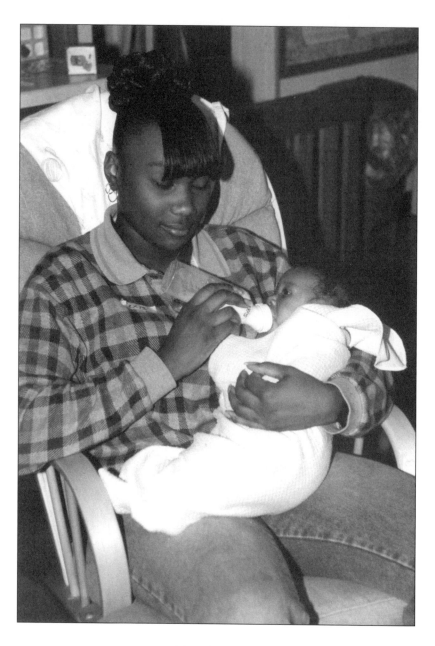

Yai and her daughter, Alexis

Yai

~

When I discovered I was pregnant, I was in denial. I didn't believe it. When my period didn't come in November of 1997, I didn't once suspect I was pregnant. I just thought my period was late. In the middle of November I bought an over-the-counter pregnancy test and it came up positive. But, for some reason, that wasn't enough. I still didn't believe I could actually be pregnant.

My boyfriend, Rashaud, kept on telling me that I was pregnant and he asked me to go to the doctor. So finally I went to the doctor in the middle of December. The test came back positive; I was stunned. I was eight weeks pregnant. I kept on asking myself, what am I going to do? Will I keep it? How would I tell my parents? And who would be there for me?

Rashaud, all my sisters, and my aunt told me to get an abortion, but by then I pretty much had my mind set that I was going to keep my child. My friends were very helpful—they just told me to make my own decision and to think about my future with and without a child. So I did. I thought that I would be a high school dropout with a child, when all I had wanted to do was get my diploma and go to college and major in journalism. I kept on thinking: graduate and go to college, or be a teen mother who has failed in life.

It turns out that having Alexis was the best thing that's ever happened to me. My daughter, Alexis, is making me push even harder to achieve the goals that I have for myself.

Andrea and her son

Andrea

~

When I was pregnant I didn't know what to do. There were so many things going on in my head—abortion, adoption, and so on. My mom said that she would pay me to get an abortion. I just couldn't go through with it. I couldn't kill this little life inside of me.

After I found out I was pregnant, I moved in with my dad and the baby's father. A lot of things started to change—my moods, my attitudes, my feelings about life. My pregnancy was hard and very emotional. Little by little, I got through it.

One day I started feeling these funny things—they were contractions. I couldn't believe it! It took me five days after I started having contractions to have my baby. I was in so much pain; I just wanted him out of me. Then again, it felt good because I was giving life. I brought a baby into the world. When he came out and I saw him, I cried. He was so tiny and beautiful. I couldn't believe he was mine.

When I took him home, it was kind of hard for his father and me. It seemed like he wanted to eat and be changed every minute. It was a big rush of responsibility. A baby is really a lot to handle, especially when you are alone. I'm very thankful that I had his father there. It was good for both of them. And I could tell that my baby loved having his dad around.

When you have a baby, you have to put the baby before yourself. I did! I can't get up and go whenever I please. His father does, and it's kind of sad because my son needs and wants both his mommy and daddy there all the time. I'm always there, but his dad is mostly out with his friends, which most dads usually do. No matter what, I know he will always be there for his son. It just hurts because he would rather stay out than be home with his family.

Now that my son is four months old, he is smiling, laughing, rolling over, and trying to crawl, and it feels so good when he does these things. When you have a baby, all the pain and emotional discomfort are worth it. I love my son more than anything in this world. He is number one in my life and he will always be.

Trisha and her son, Lucio

Trisha

~

When Lucio was born it was the best thing that ever happened to me. He's my perfect little angel. I could never live without him. His father and I aren't living together right now. I have the baby six days out of the whole week, and that one day without him I get so lonely I sometimes cry.

It's kind of hard being a parent sometimes, because if there is something going on that's really big, I have to miss it. I wish I would have waited until I finished school and college and had a house. I am living with my aunt now, because my son's father's brother went psycho on me, and I don't want my son to grow up in an unhealthy environment. I don't want my son's first word to be a cuss word. He doesn't have a crib at my aunt's house, so he's sleeping in a box. He doesn't like it very much. He still wakes up a few times in the night wanting to eat, play, or be rocked.

The only family members who help me are my aunt and my little cousin, Gigs. My son's grandma doesn't even call to see how he's doing. What really hurts is his grandpa hasn't even seen him yet. That's their fault; just because I had a baby doesn't mean they don't have anything to do with the baby. They're missing out on the most precious baby alive.

I'm going to be sad after I graduate, because I'll be leaving for the National Guard for three months. I'm doing it for my son. You can still have a future even though you have a child. It doesn't mean your life is over; there is a lot of help out there.

Lucio is eight-and-a-half months now. He doesn't have any teeth yet. He isn't crawling yet, but that's okay; otherwise, I'd be running nonstop. I can still go out and do things with school. Last week I went to the Kennedy basketball game. Lucio enjoyed it because he got to meet all the cheerleaders. Everybody wanted to hold him; he got all the attention. I'm glad. He'll be an even happier child. He's always really happy, never cries. I guess I'm pretty lucky.

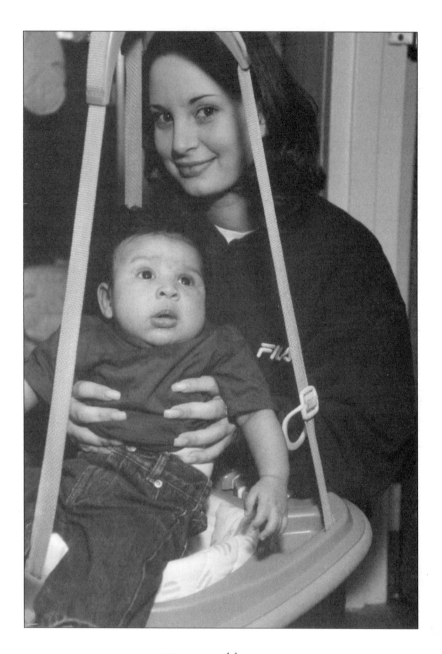

Jessica and her son

Jessica

I was a child with a child,
sixteen years old and not yet grown,
inside of my body growing a child of my own.

Here we are now, two babies crying,
and no one hears, little boy, no one hears.
Okay, hush now, I'll put away my school books;
no time for learning now I know.
Too soon I've learned of life,
not learning anything of love.
How can I teach you something I know nothing of?

For you, one lesson,
one thing I must teach you well—
to forsake what seems like small pleasure,
to guard and keep your youth while you are young.
Your youth itself is your true treasure.

For myself, one prayer,
that I may find within my adolescent frame,
the wisdom to raise you right and strong,
that I may become a woman soon,
so that you can be a child alone.

Aslener and her son, D'Andre

Aslener

~

I would like to begin by saying that being a parent is not easy. Babies are helpless and dependent on you for everything. I am lucky enough to have people around who want to help. I think the hardest part about being a parent is trying to figure out what my baby wants when he cries. Sometimes he'll cry when he isn't hungry, doesn't need a diaper, isn't tired, and doesn't have gas, and I don't know what to do.

When D'Andre was born he never cried, all he did was sleep. He was like that for about a week. Then it seemed like all of a sudden he started waking up in the middle of the night. When he woke up he wouldn't go right back to sleep; he wanted to look around and play. I think that was the hardest part, because I would have to get up in the morning for school and I'd be exhausted. But now he's starting to sleep most of the night, so it's not so bad.

If I think of D'Andre now and compare him to how he used to be, he seems like a completely different person. It seems like he's growing up so fast. It was hard to think of him as a real person before, because he never did anything. I take a lot of pride in the fact that I helped him to become this person.

People often ask me if I miss going out and being with my friends, but I feel like there isn't anything I could be doing that would give me greater satisfaction than being a parent. I'm not advising anyone to become a teen parent, because not everyone was meant to be a parent. Being a parent is not easy, but I think nothing worth doing is ever easy.

Leasa and her sons

Leasa

~

Every day is a different world; you never know who's going to be in it or what will happen.

My teenage life turned into an old lady life. It all happened when I was in eighth grade. I wanted to be like everybody else, which at the time was to be cool. My mother didn't let me go to my friends' houses, because who knew what I'd get into? I always told my mother that she never let me do anything. One day she realized I was a teenager and said, "fine." She bent her rules a little bit by letting me date this boy who went to the same school as I did. His name was Steven.

We weren't even in love—not even close. It was just a junior high experience. It was the experience of a lifetime.

Jessica

Jessica

~

My Little Angel,

There are so many things I want to say to you. First of all, when I found out that you were growing inside me, I was very excited and happy. I had a part of your daddy and me developing inside my body. Not once have I ever regretted getting pregnant. Life has been a little more challenging, but in the end it's all worth it. You are my reminder that no matter how tough it gets, there is someone making their way into the world to make it better. I remember the first time I felt you kick—it was the warmest feeling in the world. It was just a little butterfly flutter, but it made me feel so wonderful. Knowing that I am doing my part to make you grow and be healthy makes me feel that I am already being the best mommy I can be. As the months have passed I have gotten more anxious for your arrival. I can't wait to hold you in my arms and to see your beautiful smile. Your daddy and I have been getting you lots of stuff that you will need when you get here. All of your grandparents are very excited to meet you. They have been very supportive over all these months, which helps to make Mommy happy and strong for you. I just want to tell you I am sorry for the times I am not very happy. Sometimes I just get upset, but never is it because of you. You are a very important part of my life and I try my best to let you feel that. I just have about a month until you arrive. I am getting ready to go live with your daddy. I made this decision to move, so that you can receive all the love and attention you need from your daddy and me. Everyone thinks you are going to be so beautiful. They are always feeling my tummy, which is getting really big (Daddy thinks it is cute!). You are a very special part of me. I will always be here for you. If you need to talk, I am always listening. I love you with all my heart and I am going to do my best to always be the best mommy I can be. I will see you soon!

With all my love, Mommy

Monique and her daughter, MaKenzie

Monique

~

My name is Monique. I'm sixteen years old and I have a four-month-old daughter, MaKenzie. I never thought in a million years that I would be the "chosen" one. Pregnancy happened to others, but not me. When it did happen to me, I wondered, "Can I handle this?"

Now that I'm a teen parent, there's nothing better in the world than my baby girl. Every time I walk into the room her face brightens, and I feel like I'm doing my job well.

Being a teen parent isn't all fun and games, however. Sometimes MaKenzie gets overly tired, but when I lay her down, she won't go to sleep. Even if I pick her up, she's still fussy. Getting ready for school can also be hectic. First, I have to wake her up. Second, I have to get her dressed. Finally, I have to get myself dressed. These are just a few things that aren't so fun.

I like spending time with MaKenzie when we get home from school. At school we have a daycare, but there aren't many breaks during the day, so I can't go and see her that much. At home we play with her light-up toys and we play Peek-a-Boo. She's a great, enthusiastic kid.

Parenting, to me, is like a roller coaster: you have your ups and your downs. It's full of fun, excitement, fear, and disappointment. No matter how old or young a parent is, it's going to be hard. All I can say is, being a teen parent is a big responsibility.

Tara

Tara

~

When my boyfriend, Jesse, and I found out that I was pregnant, we were both shocked, but he was there for me. He told me that he still loved me and that he would not leave me. At first we both wanted an abortion, but we did not have enough money at the time to pay for it.

For the longest time I tried to forget about the baby inside of me, and so did my boyfriend. We just kept on doing the same things we always did. I started to take diet pills to try to kill the baby, but instead I was just hurting myself. Then I started to take water pills, but after a couple of days that made me feel bad, too.

Then, when I was about five-and-a-half months pregnant, I thought that the baby was dead because I had such bad pains in my lower stomach. I went to a teen clinic to get it checked out, and they said that the baby was not dead and that I had to tell my parents that I was pregnant. They also told me that I could not get an abortion because I was way too far along in my pregnancy. So that night I picked up my boyfriend and told him that we had to tell our parents. I could just tell by his face that he did not want to, but he knew that we had to. So Jesse and I went over to my house and told my mom. I could tell that she was really disappointed in me. But she said that there was nothing she could do about it now.

About a day or two later, we decided to give the baby up for adoption because we could not take care of it. Plus, we did not have enough money to raise a child. I told my mom, and she said that if Jesse and I wanted, she would adopt the baby, because she wanted another baby anyway. When my mom told my dad what she was doing, he said, "no way." So she was going to get a divorce from him, but he gave in because he did not want a divorce. But I know by the way he is acting that he does not want this baby as his own.

At about six months, I started to show a lot more because I was not taking diet pills and I was eating the way I was supposed to. So I decided to go to the South Vista school for pregnant teens. I guess in some ways it was a good thing that I changed schools. Some people at my other high school were mean to me, partly because they were not used to seeing a pregnant teen in the high school. But I miss my boyfriend and my friends.

Now that I am eight months and going to my new school, it is hard for me to see Jesse because we both work. I have gotten a lot bigger now—I weigh about 135 pounds or so. To me, I look very unattractive, but Jesse says that I "do not look bad." I still miss my friends at my old school, since I never really get to see them anymore. The baby is getting so active that I can hardly sleep at night with all the kicking and punching he does. It seems nonstop.

The thing that really gets to me is that I think Jesse does not want this baby. In the beginning he was so supportive, and now he is trying to block out the fact that he is going to be a father forever. Even if my parents are adopting it, the baby is still his. I am hoping that once the baby is born, he will come around and be nice to the baby, and love it as he would if he were taking care of his baby.

Alexandra

~

Confused

I sit in the darkness of my room, with my hands clutched tightly together. My palms sweating, my fingertips burning. I am praying, praying that this isn't true, this nightmare. How could I be so stupid? I should have told him to put one on, for heaven's sake, they were right next to us in the nightstand. My family, my friends, my school . . . what will they think of me?

Gross, Sick, Disgusting, Afraid, Depressed, Alone

That's all I can feel, all I can think of myself. I am going insane with this burden on my back. Why? Why me? Punch, punch, punch . . . over and over I punch my stomach, trying to kill what is in me, praying that I will start bleeding—then I'll know it's dead. Cigarette after cigarette, trying to suffocate what is in me. I won't say "my baby" because I don't want it. I hate it. The hunger, I have not eaten in three days, but that's good. Maybe a couple days of starvation and it will die. I must not eat until it's out.

Hiding, Locked Up, Miserable, Lying

Still living a lie. Still hiding this secret from everyone. Teachers asking, "How are you today?" "Oh, I'm fine," I say, trying to sound as jolly as I can. My mother asking, "You don't look well today, is something wrong?" "No, Mother, I'm just really tired."

Tired, Angry, Lost, Awkward

Why me? Why this? Why now? My future, it's gone. How will I finish school with a baby? My dreams, they have all been erased. What will people think? My friends, my family, my boyfriend. I wish you would get out of there—you're ruining my life, you're ruining my future.

Adoption, Abortion, Suicide

I call the father of the baby to tell him what has happened. I tell him I don't want to go through with this; I want to get an abortion. He gets very

Alexandra and her son

angry. He doesn't want me to get an abortion. He explains to me the simple fact: It's not the baby's fault it was made. We made the choice to have unprotected sex, now we need to deal with the consequences.

Confused, Without, Trapped

Days have gone by, I have had counseling and have talked about my decision. I have decided to go through with it and have MY BABY. Now all I have to do is tell my mother. I try to break it as softly as I can to my mother, but she really isn't taking it very calmly.

Silence, Mute, Quiet

A couple days go by and my mother finally talks to me. She is happy that she is going to have a grandchild, but not at the fact that I chose to have sex at a young age.

Relieved, Happy, Loved, Born Again

On September 18, 1998, I gave birth to a baby boy. He is healthy and beautiful and I thank the Lord for him every day.

I think the hardest part of finding out you're pregnant is having the guts to tell your parents. They probably have had no clue that you are sexually active, and you know they will be very disappointed because they've told you not to have sex at such a young age and, if you do, you should wear protection. The second hardest part is to tell your boyfriend, because you don't know if he will want to leave or stay, or maybe he will deny that it's his baby.

When I found out I was pregnant, I thought my future was over, but it's not; it's just beginning. Now, of course, it may be harder, but I will never give up, for my son is destined to have a bright and beautiful future, and so am I.

Melissa

Melissa

~

My Sweet Daughter,

I often ponder the teachings of life. I think about life as a training period for all humans, before we are righteous enough to know the truth. Although our time here is long, and we feel every second of every day, deep in the back of our minds we always know we've only just begun. My opinion is "everything happens for a reason." Whether you discover that reason right away, or it takes many years, there is always a reason. The many life experiences that your father and I went through were meant to teach us. No matter if they were good or bad; they helped us grow. For our own sakes, we needed them. Now we'll use our knowledge to teach you, so you can grow a little bit more than we did. Everything we do has one specific reason: you. You are all that occupies your dad's and my thoughts. As you grow inside of me, I think about what our lives together will be like. I can only hope for the best, and I can only prepare myself so much, but what God has planned is out of my hands. All I can say to you now is: I will try my best to make sure you have a loving childhood, filled with happy memories. I will also try to succeed in today's world, so you always have someone to look up to. Your dad and I love you more than anything, and we can't wait until we can hold you in our arms. Always remember one thing: No matter what happens in our lives together, nothing that you say or do can change the fact that we love you. You'll always be our little girl.

With the Deepest Love, Mom and Dad

I didn't plan on getting pregnant at this time of life. I guess, as a woman, I consider myself lucky. Mainly because the father of my baby is someone I love with all my heart, but also because my child will grow up with her father in her life. There are many misconceptions about pregnant teens. The young girls are often stereotyped. I hope I can prove many of those stereotypes wrong. Everyone in this world deserves a fair chance. I plan on getting mine, for the sake of my child, and for the future of my family.

Joyce

Joyce

~

Being pregnant has changed a lot of things in my life. My parents treat me better than they used to. My mom keeps on buying baby things, like a crib, mobile, musical night-light, clothes, etc. That helps me out a whole lot. My dad was kind of mean when he found out, but ever since he found out it was a boy, he's changed a lot. He helped me paint the baby's room, put together the crib, put new carpet in the room, and a lot of stuff like that. My mom's side of the family has been really cool with the idea of a new baby boy. My dad's side, however, isn't so enthusiastic about it.

Tony (the baby's father) is mean, period. He treats me like I'm a disease, like if he ignores me this whole thing will go away. Just yesterday I called him and he hung up on me. It hurts that he won't even talk to me anymore. We used to be real good friends until I got pregnant, then everything we had between us ended. It hurt so bad I cried in my room for at least an hour. But then I realized who and what I was wasting my tears over: a little immature boy who can do nothing but hang up the phone on a girl he helped get pregnant. I can't blame the whole thing on him; it does take two to make a baby.

His mom, Fawn, is a different story, though. She's real cool, and if I need to talk I can just call her. She even told me that she's already started to buy diapers for the baby. I'm lucky to have people who are supportive. They say that you find out who your real friends are when you're pregnant. I know I did. I don't have very many friends now, but my whole life has changed and it will never be the same again.

Nicole and her daughter, Kayla

Nicole

~

In the summer of 1995, I got pregnant with my daughter Kayla. She was born March 22, 1996. Prior to my pregnancy I had run away from home often, I experimented with a variety of drugs, and I drank a lot. The last time I ran away, I got pregnant from a statutory rape.

I moved home right away and stayed with my family. I didn't tell them that I was pregnant because of the rape. I knew that I had put myself in a bad situation. However, when I was six months pregnant, I pressed statutory rape charges against the father. He was sentenced to three years in prison when Kayla was three months old. I let my mom know what happened two weeks after Kayla was born, and I don't know if she ever told my dad.

When I was pregnant, I was afraid that I might have a boy. If he reminded me of his father I might take my anger out on my child. I worried, too, that the child might have a physical disability or deformity, and I knew I wouldn't be able to afford special care. I told God that if he wanted me to place my child for adoption, to give me a boy or a child with a disability or deformity, and if he wanted me to keep the child, to give me a healthy baby girl.

My daughter is two-and-a-half years old now and I am living with her in a transitional housing program called "Perspectives." We have a two-bedroom apartment that is close to my mother's house so I can get extra support when I need it. I am working at a good job twenty hours per week, and my school has remained a source of support. I am sober and have found new friends. I think of my daughter as my saving grace. I know that I wasn't living a healthy or safe lifestyle, and I know how I have changed. I don't know that I could have made the changes I did without having to look at the realities of an unplanned pregnancy.

My daughter is a beautiful redhead with an attitude to match. She has a good sense of humor and lots of curiosity about everything. This is not the way I would have planned my life, but I do know that I will have a better life with her in it. She reminds me of where I have come from and where I am going, and I love her for it.

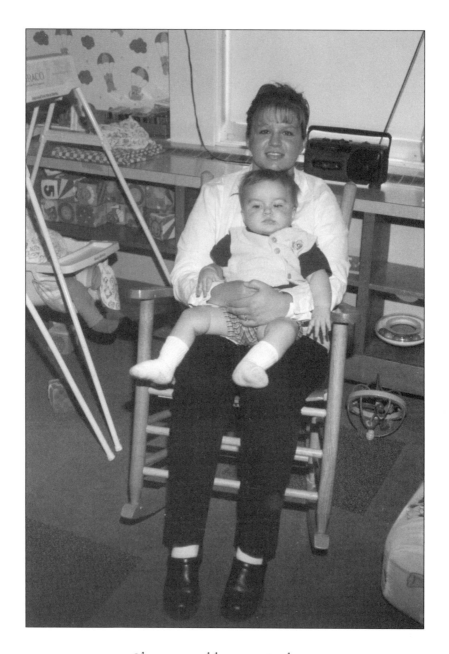

Shannon and her son, Anthony

Shannon

~

Anthony was born in August of 1998. When I looked at him I was happy, but I knew that my life was changed forever. I am very lucky; even though my parents were hurt by the fact that I was pregnant, they were very supportive. Also, my boyfriend, Jeff, was there for me, and still is. We have been together for four years.

Having a family, going to school, and going to work is very stressful for me. I am seventeen years old, and all my free time is spent with my son, Jeff, and school work. I feel like I have no time for anything else. Anthony goes to school with me, then after school I go to work. I get home around 9:00 P.M. and I talk with Jeff for about one hour out of the whole day, and then we go to bed. It is a very hard life.

I wouldn't be able to do all this on my own. I am very grateful that I have Jeff and my parents to support and help me every step of the way. If I had the choice to do it all over again, I would have waited until I finished school and had a good job. I love Anthony and Jeff very much, and I also love being a mom, but I wish I would have waited. Why rush things as a teen, when you have your whole life ahead of you?

Magnolia and her daughter

Magnolia

~

My name is Magnolia. I'm a teen mother of a five-month-old baby girl. Being a mother is not as easy as it looks. But it is also fun knowing that you are someone's mother.

Where should I start? The day before I learned I was pregnant, I took a pregnancy test and it came out negative. The test got my hopes up, because it made me think I was going to have a normal kid life, but that was just my imagination.

When I found out I was pregnant I was with my mother, and I kind of had a feeling that the test was going to come out positive, since I felt sleepy and was eating all the time. When my doctor came in, I just knew what she was going to say because the look on her face was like she had seen a ghost. "The test came out positive," she said. "What?" I said, "That can't be." Then, in a sarcastic way, she said, "Well, honey, you are." I saw the pain in my mother's eyes. I knew she just wanted to cry.

Every single dream that I had for the future died, my childhood was gone. All I could think about was, how am I going to raise this child? Would I have to drop out of school? What am I going to say to my boyfriend?

When I called to tell my boyfriend, he was totally scared and happy at the same time. What amazed me is that he wanted to see me right away. So we planned to keep the baby. Later on, when I was further along, we found jobs so we could save up for a crib and other baby stuff. That was the most exciting part of my pregnancy—knowing that I had his support, and the support of my family. That made me feel so good.

I decided to finish school, so I joined a program called South Vista Education Center, a school for pregnant teens and teen mothers. It made a big difference in my life knowing that I could still go to school and be pregnant at the same time. When I had my baby, there would be daycare provided by the school.

I had my baby shower on September 28, then I had my baby on October 2, the day after her dad's birthday. It was the happiest and scariest moment of my life. Now that I had to take care of someone and be responsible for my actions, I realized it was time to grow up.

It was really sad at the beginning because I was experiencing the baby blues. I was so depressed. I felt so sad and I was mad at myself because I had grown up too fast. When the baby was about two weeks old, she had colic symptoms—you do not know what that did to me. But everything seemed to get better over the next few weeks.

Things started to get even better when family began to help with food, diapers, and clothes. Babies are very expensive, I can tell you. That was one of the hardest parts: managing money for diapers, food, and formula.

My life with my daughter is actually better than I thought it would be. She has made me grow up and think about my actions. Even with a lot of support, it takes time to become something or someone you weren't before. That's why I'm trying my best to be a good mother.

Linda

~

I came from a really strict family; I couldn't do anything or go anywhere with my cousins or friends. Having a boyfriend or even a guy friend was out of the question. My parents thought that if they kept me away from the bad things in life, I wouldn't turn out bad. I felt trapped; the only places I went were to school and to the store with my mom. I could not attend any after-school activities. So I lied to my parents just so I could go out. To get away from all this, I ran away with my boyfriend, Kay, for three weeks.

When I came back, I started living with Kay and his family. I just couldn't live with my family at that time. I got pregnant after three months. I thought all those pains that I had been having were cramps. It was as much a shock to me as to my mom. The pill hadn't worked. I was only fifteen. What could I know about raising a child? I was a child myself.

Kay and I didn't know what we were going to do. I knew in my heart I couldn't have an abortion; I couldn't go through that. I became so depressed. My mom wanted me to have an abortion. Kay and his mom wanted me to keep the baby, but Kay knew we were too young to support a baby.

I cried every night but never showed anyone my pain. At two-and-a-half months I went to see the doctor. The baby was okay, and I still didn't know if I was going to keep it for sure. When the baby first kicked, that's when I was finally happy to have it come into my life. Kay had gotten a better job and I went to school. When we went in for an ultrasound, Kay's eyes brightened up. He saw his baby and it made him really happy. That made me happy also.

I had Kynda on April 4, 1997, at 8:13 P.M. My mom was on my left side and Kay on my right. Everyone was really supportive.

I loved Kynda from the start. I ended up in Minnesota with my mom to finish school. Kay stayed in Michigan to work. We are still together, but it's hard. I feel that school is really important and I need to graduate, not only for myself but also for Kynda. I want to set a good example for her so she won't go through what I went through. Kynda is my number one responsibility. She is nineteen months old and at the stage where she wants everything her way,

Linda and her daughter, Kynda

and it's so hard for me. I get angry sometimes because Kay's not here helping me. He calls, writes, and visits when he can, but it's not enough. Some people think it's easy to raise a child. I, myself, was one of those people. I used to babysit, and I thought that was pretty easy. I see how hard it is now.

Even though I can't take anything back, I wouldn't want to, because I can't imagine my life without Kynda. It was my mistake and I have taken on a lot of responsibility because of it; I am doing all I can. I'm closer to my family now since I had Kynda. I'm lucky to have a family that is really supportive. They love Kynda a lot. They help me with her when I go to work and when I need time away. I take Kynda with me everywhere, and that includes school. It's hard, but it is something I have to do.

I have grown up a lot since I had Kynda. One thing I learned from being a mother at such a young age is that you can't do it all alone. No matter what happens in your life, your family should always be there, so never turn away from them. Everyone makes mistakes; I know I have.

Sarah and her daughters

Sarah

~

I never thought I would get pregnant at such a young age. I am nineteen years old and a mother of two: a six-month-old and a three-year-old. I have a big responsibility now.

I get up every morning at 5:30 A.M. to get my daughters and myself ready for school. My mom helps, which I'm very grateful for. I get on the bus at about 7:30 A.M. with both my kids and their car seats, which is a big pain. When I get to school, I bring each of them to their daycare rooms, and then I go to my classes. When school is over, I get my kids from daycare and take the bus home. By this time I am tired, but my kids don't like to take naps, so I can't take one either. Since we don't take a nap, we play or find other things to do. At about 6:00 P.M. I start settling them down by giving them baths and feeding them. At 7:30 my youngest daughter goes to bed, and at about 8:30 my oldest daughter goes to bed. When they are sleeping, I get their stuff ready for the next day. After this, I try to get some homework done. At 10:30 or 11:00, I go to bed and wait for the alarm to go off.

This is what I do practically every day. I don't get to go out like I used to before I had kids. Once in a great while, my mom will watch them so I don't go crazy. But even though my life is very hectic, I wouldn't change it for the world, because I love my little girls very much.

Alice

Alice

~

When I found out I was pregnant, it put a smile on my face. I've always enjoyed being around children, and I had planned on having one of my own someday. It wasn't until later, when the consequences fell into place, that my smile faded, grim and bleak. Somewhere between "Choices" counselors and my parents finding out I was pregnant, what I had done hit me. I found myself faced with many difficult choices. For every corner I turned, there seemed to be a wall, and for every wall I ran into, there seemed to be a window, and for every window I climbed through, there was another corner. Today I'm eight months pregnant and I have two feet on the ground, but I still feel like I'm walking blindfolded through a maze. It is so easy to feel like the world is against me, as if I'm walking the wrong way down a crowded hallway.

My parents disagreed with my decision to keep my child. They shouted, "Abortion!" and threatened to throw me out of their house. I was scared, but I was stubborn, and there was no way I was changing my mind. My boyfriend insisted adoption was the answer. My relatives scorned me, ashamed, and muttered, "welfare." To them, the day I made my decision is the day I became a number. I was no longer Alice with blond hair and blue eyes, who enjoys music and has a dog named Spot. I became one more freeloader who feeds off the taxpayers' money.

Persistence and luck are the two main things that got me where I am today. I live by myself in a two-bedroom apartment and I am finishing high school. I have the resources I need to care for my child and the stamina for a bright future. I plan to attend college after high school and take education for all it is worth. I know there will be many more bridges to cross and corners to turn. For some reason I had the impression that once I got pregnant it would be a free ride; the government would just pick me up and carry me. I thought that this would be my happy ending. I wish someone would have told me otherwise.

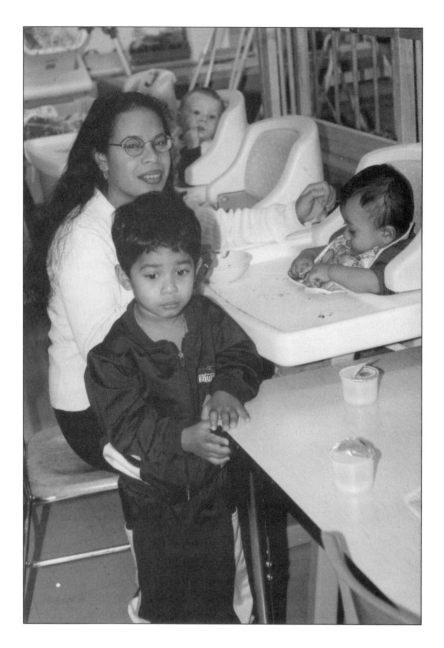

Sokha and her sons

Sokha

~

Being a teen parent is very hard. You're really not ready to be a parent and be responsible for young children. Having two children, like I do, is even harder than having one child. When you go to school, you have to dress them and bring them with you. At home, you don't really have time to concentrate on your homework. You don't have a job that pays enough money, and when you don't have enough money, it's very hard to support your children. You don't have much freedom for yourself, and if you want to go somewhere, you have to bring them along or find a babysitter. It is very hard to find a babysitter.

Being a parent is also special. You learn to take care of your children. You get to love them and be loved by them. You learn from them and they learn from you. When you have children, you feel like an adult. When they're older they can help you with anything that you need help with. And you're there to help them when they have problems. When you're sad, they can make you happy. You get to spend time with them and have fun with them. You get to teach them about what's right and wrong. When they first learn how to walk and talk, you feel proud, and your children feel proud, and they love that you are proud of them. They will do anything to get your attention. Even though it's very hard to take care of children, I really love having them and I love them very much.

Mariah

Mariah

~

When I first found out I was pregnant I thought I was dreaming. I was very scared about how my dad was going to react. Surprisingly enough, he acted totally different from what I had expected. He said, "You made the bed, now you have to lie in it." Since that day, my father has been very supportive of my choices. I'll have to live with my choices, though, for the rest of my life. It's scary, but no matter what happens, I'll always have some support.

Jessica and her daughter, Kayla

Jessica

~

Everyone thinks that being a teenager is fun and easy. You get to go out and party, have boyfriends, and never really think about the consequences of your actions. I found out I was pregnant on my sixteenth birthday. I was told to get an abortion by the father, who would rather have paid for one quick abortion than eighteen years of child support. My conscience wouldn't let me. I also thought about adoption, but that didn't feel right, either.

When the baby was born, everyone helped me with her so I could rest. Then my mom went back to work. I was home for the next five weeks taking care of this little life that cried all the time. She slept all day and was awake most of the night. I couldn't sleep during the day when she slept, because I had to work on keeping the house clean. We were selling the house, so I had to find a place for us to go whenever people were going to come through. I never got more than four hours of sleep, so I was pretty crabby.

I haven't heard from Kayla's father or received child support. I work three days a week, so I don't have much money to spend. I'm lucky that my parents buy her things. I have to pay for diapers and food, which she goes through very quickly. Hopefully, I will be getting child support soon.

When I graduate this year I can get a full-time job. Now that Kayla is getting older, I feel a little more comfortable leaving her with a babysitter, but I miss her when I'm not with her. Sometimes I worry that she thinks I am trying to dump her off on other people. It's really hard leaving her when she doesn't feel good, or when she won't let me put her down, but sometimes I have to go away.

I watch talk shows about teens who want to have a baby so they will have someone to love them. I feel bad for them. Babies can't love you back. They are selfish, in a way, although they don't do it on purpose. They want what they want, when they want it, and they are going to scream until they get it. It isn't easy to care for a baby. You have to always put the baby first. If I could do it over again, I would wait to have sex, because it would be easier to raise a baby if I wasn't one myself. No teen is ready to raise a baby, especially if she has to do it alone.

Necole

Necole

~

When I found out I was pregnant, I was shocked and didn't know what to do. At first I wanted to have an abortion, then I decided that I had to find a way to deal with the situation.

I called a friend of mine, and she told me that I needed to tell my parents, then make arrangements to see a prenatal nurse. So the next day I decided to tell one of my parents. I told my step-dad. He told me not to worry, he was going to help me tell my mom because she would have gone crazy. He told me that they had to go to the store and he was going to tell her for me. When they came back from the store, she kept asking me to do stuff for her, so I didn't know if he had told her or not. Then she asked me when I was going to tell her that I was pregnant. She told me not to worry about it, because she was going to help me take care of my baby. She told me she couldn't yell at me because she had gotten pregnant at an early age, so she wanted to be supportive of me.

The first thing we did was make a doctor's appointment. Then I had to set up a day for an ultrasound. The day of the ultrasound I had the chicken-pox, but they still wanted me to have it done. The nurse told me that I was six months pregnant and that my baby would be born on December 24.

After all the doctor appointments I was getting to the worst part: I had to tell everybody in my family, and that was going to be hard for me to do. So instead, my mom told everybody for me. They weren't disappointed in me; they just wanted to make sure that I was going to stay in school. They also wanted me to know that if there was anything I needed, I could call them and ask them to send it to me. Now I didn't have anything to worry about.

Shannon and her son, Skylar

Shannon

~

Hi, my name is Shannon. When I found out I was pregnant I was just thirteen years old. I did not know what to do or who to tell. But I decided to keep my baby. Four months later I turned fourteen. My mom had accepted the fact that I was pregnant, but she was very disappointed in me.

At sixteen weeks of gestation, the doctor told me I was going to have a little girl. At thirty-four weeks, another doctor told me I was having a little boy. At that point I had already had a baby shower, so of course I had received all girl stuff. Three weeks after the doctor figured out I was having a boy, the same doctor also found out I had toxemia. So they decided to start inducing me on Friday, November 20, 1998, at noon. But I did not have the baby until Monday, November 23, at 6:36 P.M.

It seems like ever since I had my baby, life has gone a lot smoother, even though things can get a little down once in a while. It's a lot of work to take care of a baby. I do not regret my son, but if I could do it over again, I would have waited until I was older.

My son's name is Skylar. He just turned six months old; he is very active and happy.

Jenny

Jenny

~

When I found out I was pregnant I cried my eyes out. I was so shocked and scared, I just didn't know what to do. The first thought that came into my head was, "What will my parents think?" I wished it would just go away. Well, a couple of weeks went by and I knew I had to tell my mom and my boyfriend. When I called my boyfriend and told him, he told me I was a slut and it wasn't his. That hurt me a lot; I knew it was his. Then I told my mom, and she said she had a feeling I was pregnant (mother's intuition, I guess). My mom was so supportive, she called and made a doctor's appointment to get me checked out and make sure the baby was doing okay. She also paid for the prenatal vitamins.

As the weeks went by and it started to sink in that I was really pregnant, I quit smoking and doing drugs. My friends started talking to me less and less because they all used drugs and I was sober now. By the time I got my ultrasound to find out if I was having a boy or a girl, I had no one except my parents to tell the news to. I felt so alone and worthless. So I moved in with my grandma and started going to a school for expectant mothers and teens with kids. It was so nice to go to a school where you could relate to everyone and learn about how your baby was growing inside you.

Being pregnant brought me close to my parents. It made me realize what great people they are. And my parents were happy to have their daughter back, since I was lost to drugs for so long.

As my due date got closer I became scared, thinking, did I make the right decision? Could I really handle being a mother so young? I didn't make up my mind to keep the baby until about my eighth month because it was such a life-altering decision.

I was put on bed rest for my last two months until finally, on March 22, 1999, I went to the hospital. The doctors had to induce me because I was two weeks late, and fourteen hours later I had the most beautiful baby girl. I fell in love with her the second I saw her. All I could think was—wow—I was a mother at seventeen years old.

Sarah and her daughter

Sarah

~

When I found out I was pregnant, I cried. Then I told my mom and she got mad at me because she didn't want me to make the same mistake that she did.

When I told my friends, they were happy for me, but once I had the baby, my friends said they wouldn't have any time to do things with me anymore. So my friends kind of disappeared. Now that I am out of high school, my old friends want to be friends again, but we don't do much because I have a baby, and you can't do much with a baby. But I love my child very much and won't give her up to anybody.

Kimberly and her daughter, Jealousy

Kimberly

~

I never thought something like this could happen to me, but it did. I was fifteen years old when I had unprotected sex. I know that's got to be the most stupid thing you can do at such a young age. I didn't think. I never thought I could get pregnant; things like that just didn't happen to me.

About three months later, my mom, my sister, and I drove to the clinic because I thought I had an infection. On the way my sister said, "Hope you get a girl." She meant a female doctor, because she knew I was uncomfortable about male doctors. But right when she said that, my mom and I both yelled out, "What!?" I turned around and asked, "Why did you say that?" My mom looked at me and asked if I was pregnant. I was pretty sure I was, because I was late, and I'm never late. "I think so," I told her. I was so scared.

When we got to the clinic, my sister stayed in the car. My mom told the doctor I needed a pregnancy test. When they were finished, we waited in a small room for the nurse to come in with the results. When she walked in with the doctor, they started talking about what I should do for the infection. I didn't even want to hear about it; I wanted to know if I was pregnant or not.

Finally, she said, "And about the pregnancy test. . . ." Right when she said, "It's positive," I broke out in tears. I was mad at myself for being so stupid. Everybody kept saying that everything was going to be okay.

I waited in the car while my mom talked to the doctor. My sister asked me what was wrong, but she already knew. I didn't feel like talking to anyone.

When my mom came out, she told me she would stand by me, no matter what my decision was. She told me she didn't believe in abortion, but that it was my choice. I was so confused. I didn't believe in abortion either, but I didn't feel ready to have a baby.

After a while, I knew I couldn't bring myself to kill an innocent baby. I decided to go through with the rest of the nine months. It never actually hit me that there was a living person inside until I felt the first kick. My doctor wanted me to get an ultrasound to determine how far along I was. I went with my boyfriend. When we saw the little baby on the blurry screen, we couldn't believe it. They showed us a picture of its feet. It looked like there were about ten toes on each foot. I knew my baby would be perfect. We didn't know the sex of the baby just yet, so we agreed to wait until the end to find out.

I thought my boyfriend was going to leave me, but we actually became closer. I give him credit for putting up with all my emotions. I've never cried so much or gotten so angry in my whole life. It was pretty crazy. We went out a lot; he was so nice to me, even though I was acting different.

It was Friday, over a week past my due date, and I was going to be induced on Monday. My doctor had told me to walk a lot and to drink more fluids. That day, my boyfriend and I walked over to Applebee's for lunch. About halfway through my meal, I started having contractions. I thought it was nothing, because I'd had contractions before and they were always nothing.

I wanted to get a car seat that day, so we asked for the bill and walked over to Target. My boyfriend insisted on getting the most expensive car seat they had. Just then my contractions started getting stronger. People in the store looked at me funny, because I was walking really slowly and I was in pain.

We called for a taxi and went to my boyfriend's house. I laid on the bed and waited for the contractions to stop. My sister came over and saw me in pain. She told me to call Mom, but I kept telling her they would go away soon. About ten minutes later, the pain was really bad. I told my sister to call my mom and tell her I was ready for sure this time.

My mom picked us up and took us to the hospital. When we got there, they made me walk around to make the contractions stronger. They told me I could sit down whenever I needed to. I was down on the ground with every contraction. I couldn't believe the pain. Nothing ever hurt so badly in my life. I didn't even know how I was supposed to breathe, but one of the nurses showed me what to do. I felt like I was going to die.

I was in labor for twelve hours before they told me I could push. When the baby came out, they laid it on my stomach so my body heat would keep it warm. I cried. I couldn't believe this was my little creation. This was what I had made.

I asked the doctor if it was a boy or a girl. "It's a girl," he told me. She was perfect. I knew that one day everyone would be jealous of her. Her name had to be Jealousy Tears. Tears, because every time I looked at her I cried. It's been hard, but I can't deny the fact that I love her so much.

Molly

~

I hope my story will better educate others on exactly what teen parenthood is all about, the good and the bad. I also hope it will encourage those who wish to have sex at a young age to reconsider their decision, so they will be able to avoid what I and many others have gone through.

I became pregnant at age fifteen by a man who was only seventeen. We, like many others who are inexperienced, thought we were in love. He proved to be a violent and selfish man who was just interested in sex, drugs, and booze. To me, however, he knew just what to say to make me think he was "Mr. Perfect."

During my pregnancy, my parents and I took on all the bills, including medical and other necessities required for a newborn. The father only came around when he needed money for his own pleasure. Once my daughter was born on August 10, 1997, the bills started coming in for everything you could imagine. They came straight to me. To this day, he still has not given me any child support, only a lot of physical and emotional pain and agony.

I finally took a stand and broke up with him on Christmas day of 1997. I never felt so free in my life. Even though Jamie couldn't say anything at the time, I know she was grateful for my decision.

Since then, I have accomplished so much for the benefit of us both. I have been able to keep up an "A" average in school, and also take classes in college to become a nursing assistant. I found a job that earns me $12.37 an hour, and that has helped immensely. However, it will never eliminate all the obstacles that will come my way for the next eighteen years.

I guess the main thing I want my readers to understand is not to always trust what a man tells you, even if it's exactly what you want to hear. If he really loves you, he will wait until both of you are old enough and mature enough to be parents, in case that happens. Of course, for religious reasons, it is always better to wait until you are married.

Being a teen mother isn't at all easy, and most often, the father will not be there for you during the hard times. You will often feel very alone and

Molly and her daughter, Jamie

unsure of what to do next. I was lucky to have such a supportive family to stand by my side when my boyfriend wouldn't.

Every time I look at my daughter, I see the angel that God sent down from heaven for me. I have been blessed with a beautiful, healthy daughter. I owe her and God so much for totally turning my life around, and giving me new goals and hope for the future.

If you do happen to become a mother or father at a young age, remember to put your child first. Think of the pregnancy as a blessing in disguise rather than a curse. Maybe somebody up above is letting you know that you need to slow down and rethink your priorities.

Nicole and her son, Cody

Nicole

~

Like most sixteen-year-olds, I was looking forward to graduating in a couple of years. But then I found out that I was pregnant. What a shock! What was I going to do? What was going to happen?

Although I knew there was a possibility that I could be pregnant, I lied to my friends and told them I wasn't. Mainly, I didn't know what I wanted to do about my pregnancy.

Eventually, I decided to continue with my pregnancy, still not knowing what I was going to do. I knew that I wouldn't be able to support the baby on my own. Well, July 5, 1996, came around and that is when I had the baby. I named him Cody.

The first couple of months were really weird. I didn't know what to do when he cried; I didn't even know how to hold him right. My mom was there for Cody and me. She helped me support Cody and would even babysit on the weekends when I needed a break.

I got really frustrated at times, and I wanted to yell and scream when I didn't know what to do.

I went back to school right away and had to find a babysitter to watch Cody while I was at school. My senior year I came to South Vista Education Center. Cody liked being in the South Vista daycare with all of the other kids.

Every morning I get up at 6:30 A.M. and take a shower. Then I get dressed and brush my hair. At 6:45 I get Cody up; change his diaper; get him dressed; put his socks and shoes on; get his coat, hat, and mittens on; and leave to go to school.

Being a teen parent is really hard because you have all of this responsibility and no freedom. Some people think it's all fun and games; well, it's not. Take it from me, I know.

Shanna and her son

Shanna

~

As I sit here writing and looking back on my life, I realize that I would not change a thing. I found out I was pregnant at the age of fifteen. The day was Memorial Day of 1997. It was a day that changed my life forever. In nine months I would be a mother and be responsible for a whole other life besides my own. Wow! did I grow up fast after that day. I switched schools in the fall, the beginning of my junior year. I no longer went to a regular high school and did things "normal" teenagers do. I went to a school for pregnant teens and teen moms. Along with my normal math, English, and science classes, I was required to take a parenting class. My friends and I began to grow apart because we no longer had anything in common. While they were worrying about the latest fashions and what to wear for their dates on Saturday night, I was deciding whether to breast or bottle feed.

Telling my family the news was probably the hardest thing I have ever had to do. Both my mom's sisters yelled at me and basically demanded that I get an abortion. My mom stood by my side the whole way and supported every decision I made. I don't know how I would've gotten through this without her.

I never knew how much being pregnant affected a woman's life, but I learned quickly. I had to change my diet and eat healthier for my baby. I quit smoking. I slept as much as I could. I had to go to the bathroom every five minutes. I no longer went out with friends on the weekend. My weekends were spent working and sleeping. I lived like an old lady.

The day my son was born was the happiest day of my life. The moment I saw him and held him in my arms, I knew that there was no greater love in the whole world.

My life certainly has changed—in some aspects, for the better. I don't have the freedom most teenage girls have. I do have motivation, and I work very hard both at work and in school to give my baby the best life I can. If I feel like giving up, I think of him, and I know I will do whatever it takes to make his life great. My weekends consist of working, caring for my son, and sleeping, but I would not change a thing. My son is my life and my heart, and I wouldn't give him up for the world.

Stephanie and her son

Stephanie

~

It was the middle of my junior year. Soon enough I would be a senior. I was looking forward to senior prom, turning eighteen, and going to college out of state to become a teacher.

The day before Christmas I found out I was pregnant. At least, according to a home test. Disbelief and depression set in. What was I going to do? What would people think of me? And the biggest question of all, what would my family say? I decided to wait until after Christmas and take another test. It came back positive. I was scared. I felt as if my life was over. I thought my plans for the future were destroyed. I wondered, should I get an abortion? No, I could not live with myself if I did that. When I finally did tell my family, they were very supportive.

My aunt told me that everything would be fine as long as I trusted in the Lord. I held on to those words throughout my pregnancy. Making the decision to keep my son was the best choice that I have made in my life. I fell in love with him the moment I laid my eyes on him. Becoming a mother did not destroy my goals; it has helped me become more focused. I have never known a love like the one that I have for my son. I am working hard to create the best future possible for both of us. I know that if I keep my faith in God, all things are possible.

Julie and her son

Julie

~

At the age of seventeen, I decided to rebel against my parents, as I had done many times before. But this time was different. Instead of chasing after me, they decided to just let me go. I thought I knew it all, so I dropped out of school and moved out. My mother kept telling me not to have a baby, that it wasn't all fun and glamorous, but I took it upon myself to ignore her wisdom.

Well, once I thought I was going to make it on my own, I became pregnant. I decided for the next two months I would continue to live on my own in order to prove something to my family. I thought my friends would support me; however, this didn't happen and my family stepped in.

Being a teen parent is difficult, but for every lost soul there is a found one. My son is a growing boy and I love him dearly. The struggle will become less intense as the years go by. I watch and wonder how other teen mothers do it without family support. I never could have.

Children are mysteries; their thoughts just float around like all the other dreams in the world. If you think it is easy for your friends who are pushing strollers and being parents, please buy a doll first. The responsibilities are endless. Believe it or not, your parents are more often right than wrong.

The Partners

～

South Vista Education Center

In the early 1970s, pregnant high school students who kept their babies had two options: They could drop out of school, or they could meet with a tutor four to six hours a week to continue their education. Many of these teenagers married early or placed their children for adoption.

At this time, three educators from Robbinsdale, Minnesota, met with the superintendent of the newly formed Intermediate School District 287 (a consortium of thirteen suburban school districts). They hoped to establish a small high school that would serve pregnant teens from all thirteen districts.

In January 1972, a new program—Continuing Education Centers (CECs) North and South—opened its doors at two locations in the Twin Cities. The North CEC was located in Brooklyn Park, the South CEC in Bloomington. Both schools were housed in apartment complexes, which provided a cozy, homelike atmosphere.

Students brought their own lunches and provided their own transportation. During the six-and-a-half-hour school day, they studied English, math, science, social studies, business, home economics, and child development. At last, pregnant teens and teenage parents could complete their education in a caring, supportive atmosphere.

At the South CEC, which later became South Vista Education Center, Bloomington Division of Public Health provided onsite nursing care for its pregnant students and new mothers. A public health nurse met with students (individually and in groups) for six to eight hours a week, offering nutrition counseling, prenatal classes, preparation for labor and delivery, family planning assistance, and more.

Soon, support groups were established for couples and for the students' parents, and guest speakers presented weekly lectures on topics selected by the students. Social workers offered counseling to help with parenting and adoption decisions.

By 1975, each school district in Intermediate District 287 provided bus service to CECs North and South. Students maintained close ties to their home schools, and each graduated from her home school after completing the required credits.

Over the next several years, CECs North and South moved to new locations: Robbinsdale Community Center in Robbinsdale, and Lincoln Hills Center in Richfield. But as the program continued to grow, changing demographics presented an unmet need. More and more students were keeping their babies, and students began dropping out of school for lack of childcare. To address this problem, District 287 and Hennepin County Community Services combined efforts to provide quality onsite daycare for the children of teen parents. The new program was called Parent-Infant Education (PIE) North and South. Each site was licensed to care for fifteen infants and toddlers.

Between 1985 and 1992, the programs continued to grow, serving approximately 100 students and 75 children at each site per year. Eventually, a PIE West program was established to serve teen parents in the western suburbs.

In 1994, North CEC formed a partnership with Minneapolis Public Schools and North Memorial Medical Center to establish the North Vista Education Center. In 1997, South CEC formed a similar partnership with Fairview Health Services, founding the South Vista Education Center.

Because of these partnerships, pregnant teens and teenage parents have access to a higher level of education, prenatal care, daycare, and social service support, as well as transportation, breakfast and lunch programs, mentors, extensive career counseling, and job shadowing opportunities.

NANCY BENGSTON, MA
Former facilitator at South Vista Education Center

Bloomington Division of Public Health

Pregnant adolescents are at high risk for premature labor and other complications. In addition, they often face social and economic concerns that directly affect their health, including excessive stress, poor nutrition, inadequate healthcare, and financial problems. To protect the health of teen mothers and their babies, the Bloomington Division of Public Health provides daily nursing services to students attending the South Vista Education Center.

The public health nurses at South Vista maintain a friendly and respectful open-door policy, providing nursing care, individual counseling, and assistance in locating community resources. We teach weekly prenatal classes on pregnancy, diet and exercise, labor and delivery, breastfeeding, infant care, adoption, postpartum family planning, and other topics. New mothers also learn about child safety, medical care, immunization schedules, childhood illnesses and injuries, normal growth and development, and other childcare issues. In addition, all children in daycare are screened regularly to make sure they are developing properly.

Every year, 100 percent of our pregnant students receive prenatal care, and 100 percent of the children in daycare are brought up to date with their immunizations. Over the last five years, 92 percent of students who gave birth had children with birth weights over 5 1/2 pounds. In the state of Minnesota, the goal is to increase the number of normal birth-weight babies to 97 percent by 2004.

National statistics indicate that 20 percent of adolescent pregnancies are repeat pregnancies. Therefore, one of our priorities is to help our students remain pregnancy-free. We offer counseling, contraceptives, monthly pregnancy tests, and frequent questionnaires to help identify and solve problems that could lead to further unplanned pregnancies—lack of health insurance, lack of transportation to medical appointments, problems managing medications and contraceptives, fear and uncertainty in relationships, and other concerns.

Each month, we make a point of acknowledging and celebrating students who remain pregnancy-free. In recent years, the repeat-pregnancy rate has been as low as 0 percent.

Bloomington Division of Public Health removes a significant obstacle toward self-sufficiency for teenage mothers. By providing onsite health services, we help ensure the health of both mother and baby. When healthcare is no longer an obstacle, students are able to focus on the future: remaining pregnancy-free, completing their education, becoming good parents, and supporting themselves and their children.

Rose Jost, RN, PHN, MEd
Bloomington Division of Public Health

Fairview Health Services

At Fairview Health Services, our mission is to improve the health of the communities we serve, both within and beyond the walls of our hospitals and clinics. Sometimes, this means more than providing medical care: Research shows that poverty and lack of education lead to an increased risk of poor health, injury, and death. Therefore, as a corporate sponsor of South Vista Education Center, we are working to help teen parents finish school so they can support themselves and their children.

In partnership with Intermediate School District 287 and Bloomington Division of Public Health in Bloomington, Minnesota, we strive to ensure healthy pregnancies and healthy full-term babies. We encourage young mothers to stay in school and avoid further pregnancies. We help provide funding for daycare, housing, and other services. But our long-term goal is to help these girls develop a positive vision for their future. We want each young mother to look five, ten years down the road and see herself as a successful, independent adult. We have found that, once a young mother can clearly envision the person she wants to become, her behavior begins to support that vision. If she can see herself as a high school or college graduate with a steady, well-paying job in a field she loves, she will begin to focus on academic achievement. If she can envision having a healthy, happy family—even if her own parents were abusive or neglectful—she will work to become a stable, loving parent to her child.

To help teen mothers develop a positive vision for the future, Fairview has established a Teen Mentor Program. The mentors are Fairview employees—successful, self-sufficient women who serve as important role models. Each mentor meets with her student every other week throughout the school year to discuss the student's strengths, skills, and interests. The mentors encourage the students to stay in school, helping them to identify potential careers and to explore work and training opportunities that will further their goals.

Through our mentoring program, we've watched the young mothers of South Vista develop social confidence, clarity about their interests, and plans for their future. In exchange, we've gained a profound respect for their courage and perseverance in overcoming the challenges of teen motherhood.

Fairview is a community-focused health system providing a complete range of services, from preventing illness and injury to caring for the most complex medical conditions. These services are provided in many settings, including community centers, homes, clinics, hospitals, and long-term care centers. Headquartered in Minneapolis, Minnesota, Fairview is a not-for-profit organization affiliated with the University of Minnesota.

The mission of Fairview Health Services is to improve the health of the communities we serve. We commit our skills and resources to the benefit of the whole person by providing the finest in healthcare, while addressing the physical, emotional, and spiritual needs of individuals and their families.

Hennepin County

To obtain full-time employment that pays a livable wage, education is essential. But many young mothers who hope to complete their education face a significant obstacle: lack of childcare. Without adequate childcare, teen mothers may be forced to drop out of school.

To help these students stay in school, Hennepin County of Minnesota purchases daycare services on behalf of the students at South Vista Education Center. The daycare is located onsite, so students are able to bring their children with them to school. Daycare professionals provide a safe and stimulating environment to aid child development, and each student is required to volunteer at the daycare to improve her parenting skills.

When we make teen parents a priority—when we invest in the future of these young people—we begin to break the cycle of poverty and dependence that can damage families and drain community resources. By providing subsidized childcare today, we help these young women succeed in the long run as they earn their diplomas, follow their ambitions, and learn to support themselves and their families.

KAREN HOGLUND

Contract manager, Children and Family Services, Hennepin County, Minnesota

306.874   Daycare and
DAY   diplomas.

33035000440278

$9.95

DATE			

BAKER & TAYLOR